WINNING STRATEGIES FOR EFFECTIVE CLIENT ONBOARDING

EMERY V. BROWN

TABLE OF CONTENTS

CLIENT ONBOARDING

Did you know that clients are three times more likely to leave during their first 90 days of using your service?

Having a good client onboarding strategy is one of the most important things you can do to reduce churn and make sure the relationship you're starting with the client is a productive and profitable partnership.

It doesn't really matter what type of service you're providing, whether you're a fitness coach or a digital agency; a good client onboarding workflow is imperative. A positive onboarding experience lets the client know that they made a good choice and helps retention rates.

There are two reasons that customers churn:

- **They're not getting any value from your product/service**
- **They don't understand your product/service**

Your customers already like you and see value in your product. That's why they bought it. Sometimes it just takes a little hand holding as they get started. You can achieve this by ensuring that their experience after the sale is positive and that you fulfill the promises you made.

Onboarding doesn't always start with a purchase. **It can start the first time a lead comes into contact with your brand.**

Let's dig into everything you need to know about client onboarding and look at actionable ways you can improve your process.

What Is Client Onboarding?

Onboarding is a way of nurturing new customers and getting them acquainted with your product. Exceptional customer onboarding includes support, helpful guidance, and tutorials so they can achieve success using your product or service.

Remember, your clients are new to your service and will come with all different types of experiences. Some might be comfortable just diving in while others might be a little bit nervous, both about using your product and whether they've made a good decision about their investment in you.

The onboarding process is intended to start a relationship with the client that will introduce them to your brand, products, and services, while also building a mutually beneficial and lasting relationship.

Really great client onboarding gets your new client up to speed and addresses any questions they have before they even have to ask them. You want them to feel like they've made a great choice and that you will be solving the problems that they came to you for in the first place.

The Importance of Client Onboarding

A solid onboarding process for new customers has major benefits for your customer and for your business.

Onboarding simplifies your customer's life because all of the information they need to use

your products or service is accessible to them right away. It allows them to go through the process seamlessly and creates feelings of trust in your business.

It's important to your business for essentially the same reason. If you've already given new customers all the knowledge they need to get started, that's less time that you have to spend answering their questions and teaching them how to use your service or product.

Onboarding sets the tone for the relationship with your new customer. In addition, it increases Customer Lifetime Value (CLV), reduces churn, and turns your new customer into a fan who will probably sing your praises to all of their friends and colleagues.

Onboarding provides a ton of value to you and your client:

- It's easier to sell to an existing client than it is to find a new one.
- Most revenue comes from existing customers.

- Clients are most likely to churn in the first 90 days. Having an onboarding process in place builds your relationship and demonstrates value early on.

- When customers are happy, they will tell the world about it. Clients like when there is a clear plan of action and they feel confident in your abilities. They will become your top referral sources.

- By setting expectations early, you can reduce scope creep, which will have you doing extra work for no extra money.

- You can upsell with ease when you have a well-executed onboarding process because you've delighted your customers early on.

- Onboarding will increase customer retention, which can lower acquisition costs and increase your revenue.

A great onboarding strategy improves customer retention and helps to grow your business.

CREATING AN ONBOARDING STRATEGY

Your onboarding process sets the tone for the relationship you build with your customer. Happy customers will refer other customers, as well as purchase from you again.

Creating an onboarding strategy allows you to put much of the process on autopilot. If there's no strategy, your business could suffer with more churn and ineffective marketing.

Before you create anything that the customer is going to see, first develop a goal for your onboarding process and then make plans for how to get there.

As you start to build out your onboarding strategy, your objectives should stay specific to your products and customer base. Naturally, you'll refine this as you learn more about your customers and are able to gather more data.

Whatever objectives you have, make sure they address these retention goals:

- Encourage the customer to use your product more than once in the first week
- Establish a pattern of usage
- Make sure the client finds your product indispensable

Some of the data that you previously gathered on your target audience during the marketing and sales processes can carry over into the initial stages of onboarding. Gathering this information together gives you the best shot at having a successful onboarding experience.

Keep in mind that though you have significant amounts of data about your prospects, they only have one impression of you. This makes onboarding all that more important.

Onboarding Objectives

Client onboarding is part of the buyer's journey. Seeing it as a journey and not a destination is a great way to approach setting goals for your onboarding process. Onboarding is where the foundation for your relationship is laid. Putting the time into building a solid foundation will create a happy, long-lasting relationship with potential for upsells, future sales, and referrals.

Depending on your particular business, your goals may be different, but essentially, they should look something like this:

- **Education:** You want to understand your client and find out what they want out of the relationship. If this is a B2B relationship, learn about their business and what their objectives are for your product. If it's a coaching client, find out what they are hoping to achieve through your relationship. Remember to discover their pain points.

- **Integration:** They need to know how to utilize your product and you need to know what knowledge they need to be successful.

- **Expectations:** Set very clear expectations for the relationship. Let them know where they can find information they need and what your availability is for personally helping them.

- **Timeline:** Create a timeline for different portions of the onboarding project. Include onboarding and post onboarding.

- **Project goals:** Outline the agreed upon goals for your project. Make sure everyone is on the same page.

When both you and your client know what to expect from the relationship, everything will run much more smoothly.

As with any relationship, setting clear expectations from the start is the key to success.

These are some common areas where customer relationships can go awry if they aren't clearly defined in the onboarding process:

- **Response time:** Clearly state to your new client an expected response time for any inquiries they might have. For example, within 24 hours, Monday through Friday.

When the client knows the response time,

they are less likely to panic and send multiple emails and make dozens of calls. Of course, some types of businesses may need to be available on an emergency basis. The bottom line is that laying out these guidelines and expectations early on keeps communication running smoothly.

- **Timeline:** Clearly define the timeline, both for onboarding and during the execution of the project or service. It's your responsibility to explain your process to the client so they aren't surprised by a lack of external momentum.

  If your job entails research and strategy development, they need to know that so they aren't agitated when they don't "see" things getting done.

- **Transparency:** Make sure you have a plan in place to keep the client updated on your progress, what obstacles are being encountered, what's working, and what's not working. Let them know how this will be done and when, whether it's biweekly phone calls or daily emails.

- **Responsibilities:** Client relationships are two-sided. You and the client must be committed to follow through on your responsibilities. Outline responsibilities for both of you right from the beginning and review them often. There's nothing worse than a project being delayed because someone wasn't clear about their responsibilities.

Creating an Onboarding Workflow

Before you dig in and start creating your onboarding process, it might be helpful to create a workflow of what needs to happen when. Creating a workflow for this process allows you to map out what your onboarding process will look like.

Keep in mind, there's a lot of software available out there that can help you automate significant portions of this process. The outlines below are for a very basic workflow. They are a great jumping off point and you can add and rearrange them once you get started.

Example 1:
Workflow for freelancer or individual professional.

1. Welcome Email
2. Contract
3. Payment
4. Questionnaire
5. Meeting

Example 2:
Workflow primarily for coaching businesses.

1. Query
2. Discovery Call
3. Follow-Up
4. Invoice
5. Payment
6. Contract
7. Onboarding Forms
8. Schedule Call
9. Notes & Documents
10. Evaluation & Testimonials

Example 3:
Workflow for SaaS products.

1. Welcome Email
2. Greeting Message
3. Setup
4. Feature Callout

5. Interactive Walk-Through
6. Knowledge Base
7. Routine Check-In
8. Celebration Pop-Up

HOW TO ONBOARD NEW CLIENTS

The point of having an onboarding process for your new clients is so they can get acquainted with your product or, so you can get acquainted with them and their goals.

For example, if you're a health or financial coach, you may need to spend more time on client questionnaires so you know where your client is starting so you can set them on an appropriate path.

Client Intake Process

Let's walk through some of the steps your clients may take during their intake process. While everyone's process will be a little different, you may find some things that you just hadn't thought of yet for your own business.

1. Contract and payment. First things first, you need to have a signed contract or engagement letter and you need to get paid. If you're selling a product with a one-time payment or access to a program, you may or may not need a contract. Consult with an attorney to find out what your liability is.

This process might look something like this:

- Create a **proposal,** then get it signed by the client and returned to you.
- Build the **contract** with all of the specifics.
- Send your **invoice.**
- **Follow up** for signed contract and payment.

2. Welcome email. Be sure your first correspondence with your new customer is positive and reassuring. You want to congratulate them on making the decision to start on this path with you and thank them for choosing you. Reiterate how excited you are to be working with them.

If they need to create a login and password for your website, you might provide a link to do that.

Remember, one of your goals is to get them using your product or service multiple times. If you can redirect them back to the product, that will help you in achieving that goal.

Maybe have them log in and complete a task to get a free checklist or some other type of bonus.

3. Greeting message. This is different from a welcome email as it is generally an in-app message to greet the user the first time they log in. The goal is to get them started setting up their account and interacting with your product. Ask your client to complete a task while there, such as turn on notifications or change their password.

It's also a great place to insert an introductory video with explanations of features or your brand story.

4. Client onboarding questionnaire. Next, you need to ensure that you have all of the information you need to get started with your new client. This could look really different depending on your business and what services you're providing.

For example, if you're a coach of some kind, you'll want to know what the client hopes to accomplish with your services. You'll also want to know what their limitations are, what made them seek out coaching services, etc.

If you're a freelance copywriter, you'll want to know about the clients' brand voice, tone, what their products do, and what they're hoping to accomplish with your copywriting.

Here is some other potential information you could collect:

- Who will be the main point of contact?
- What are your goals for this relationship?
- Have you used a service like mine in the past?
- What other methods have you tried to achieve your goals?

Essentially, this is where you get the information you need to be successful in helping the client achieve their goals.

5. Client kickoff meeting. Depending on your particular business, this might not be necessary. This is where it all gets going. Everyone is excited and ready to get started. This meeting is where you can build some rapport with your client and/or their team and set the tone for the rest of the engagement.

Here are a few of the things you should cover during this meeting:

- Introductions
- Client goals
- Deliverables and responsibilities (including a timeline for both)
- The scope of your services and how scope creep will be handled
- Next steps
- Answering questions and concerns

By the end of this meeting, you will ideally have a good rapport started with the client, have answered the clients questions and had your questions answered, and outlined how the project will proceed forward.

6. Welcome package. Next, you want to make sure that your client gets some sort of welcome package from you. It's a great opportunity to provide education to the client and reinforce their decision to work with you. A little effort here can go a long way to build loyalty and reduce churn.

Your welcome package could be a mixture of physical products as well as digital assets. Here are some ideas to help you get started:

- **A "cheat sheet":** This is information that your client can print out and should include any information they would need about your business. For example, business hours, contact information, emergency contact numbers, typical response times, and FAQs.

- **Case studies:** Toot your own horn a bit and share some positive results you've gotten with other clients in the past. This helps to build trust with the client and helps them to feel like they made a good decision.

- **Homework:** What resources will your client need in order to get the most out of your relationship? Maybe link to a content library or an outline of how you are going to help them achieve their goals.

- **Welcome video:** Creating a welcome video is a great way to get your clients fired up and excited about working with you.

- **Swag:** Everyone loves a free gift, so take advantage of that fact and get something physical into their hands that reminds them of the relationship you're building.

The welcome packet is going to accomplish two things:

- Set expectations for the onboarding process
- Reinforce their decision to buy your product or service

Another helpful thing you can include with your welcome packet is a timeline for the next steps they need to take next as well as what they can expect from you.

7. Checkup call. About 30 days after you start working with a client, schedule a call to check in and make sure everything is working smoothly. If you're a coach and have many clients, this could also go out in an email. However, if you really want your clients to feel like you're in it with them, a phone call is best.

Remember, the first 90 days is the window for building a good first impression of your company.

This is when you want to catch any problems and solve them moving forward. It's also a great way to give your client a nudge if they haven't given you information or documents that you need.

CLIENT ONBOARDING BEST PRACTICES

As you build out your client onboarding process, there are a few key points that you'll want to keep in mind.

Understand Your Customer

Your buyer personas are going to be key to understanding your customers. Well-defined personas will allow you to understand every obstacle they face, each pain point they endure, and what they're looking for in a solution.

Buyer personas are semi-fictional representations of your target customers. They are created using data and research either from your own customer base or from that of your competition. Personas aid in finding qualified prospects, guiding product development, and aligning all aspects of your organization from marketing to onboarding.

Personas are important information to have and well worth the time and effort you'll put into creating them. Personas will help you to personalize your client onboarding experience.

Set Clear Expectations

Before the customer purchases your product or signs a contract with you, they should know exactly what to expect. Your sales process should educate them about any qualifying factors for using your product or service.

Your onboarding process should reiterate the value the consumer is getting with your product and prepare them for any problems they might have, as well as how to deal with them.

This is also a good time to set boundaries. Let the client know when you are available, when you're not, and where they can find answers to commonly asked questions.

Demonstrate Value

In order to get your customer excited about your product and keep them delighted with their purchase, you need to take every opportunity you can to reemphasize the value it will provide.

Use specific examples of how your product or service will help. A specialized email, training, or call would be a great way to accomplish this.

Stay in Regular Communication

After your initial welcome email, continue reaching out to your new client using email throughout the entire onboarding process. Depending on your business, you could set this up through your Customer Management System (CMS) to trigger when they complete certain tasks. You could also set up other emails to trigger if they don't complete certain tasks within a certain time frame.

This will help you to keep the client on track and coming back to your product. Once your product becomes something they use on a regular basis, you can back off with the emails and rely more on in-app notifications.

Keep Your Approach People-Focused

Keep in mind that one size doesn't fit all. Try to customize your service or product as much as possible. A people-focused approach will help you to be more attentive to each client's specific goals and needs.

When you focus on people, you can acknowledge their fears and concerns while also answering their questions. This is a huge part of building trust with your clients. Keep track of concerns that the client has and revisit those concerns to make sure they are addressed.

Most of all, just remember that your clients are people, not just sales. Create goals that are customer-centric. You want your client to have goals that are unique to their situation. Allow them to define success for themselves and then help them to create measurable milestones to get there.

Each client has unique concerns. Tailoring your solutions to their needs will allow you to achieve big wins and create loyal customers.

Other Best Practices to Keep in Mind

Don't ask for a million things at once. Don't overwhelm your new client by asking them for everything you need from them all at once. This is a sure-fire way to drive them away. Onboarding is a journey best taken at a slow and steady pace. Keeping your information requests simple will help to move your client through the onboarding process while also keeping them engaged.

Disseminate information slowly and in an orderly way. Request information based on where they are in the onboarding process. Only ask them to accomplish one task at a time and provide them with clear instructions.

Seek positive interactions. Your goal is to give the customer the same positive experiences that made them sign on with you in the first place.

Measure your success. A great onboarding process benefits both your client and your business. Gather feedback from your customers and identify places in your process that could use a little extra work.

EMAIL SEQUENCES FOR ONBOARDING NEW CLIENTS

As you might have guessed, many businesses will be able to do most of their onboarding through email sequences.

When your clients first purchase your product or service, they want to know how to get the most value out of it. Sending random or promotional emails isn't going to endear them to you and turn them into loyal brand advocates.

This is even more true if your onboarding process starts when they sign up for your email newsletter, subscribe to your blog, or take advantage of a lead magnet. If this is the case, you'll want to create an email sequence that nurtures them to conversion.

Effective onboarding emails can be the start of a positive customer experience.

Benefits of Email Onboarding

An engaging email sequence can be your secret weapon to building long-lasting relationships with your new clients. Here are two primary reasons email onboarding can be a real boost for your business.

1. Engages new clients. Email is an extremely popular and well-used communication channel. More than half of the world's population has an email account.

Clients love email because they can get promotional content, reach out for support, and get notifications to keep them up-to-date on product and service related news.

2. Creates lifetime customers. Having loyal customers who stick by you throughout their customer journey is a key component in your business succeeding. Loyal customers minimize churn and retaining customers is far less expensive than constantly trying to acquire new ones.

Welcoming new clients and subscribers is the perfect first step in turning them into loyal customers. A well-designed onboarding sequence makes a great first impression.

If you don't greet your new subscribers and clients right away, they may be left with the impression that they are on their own or that you were only interested in selling products, not developing a relationship.

Welcoming them after the sign-up lets them know that you're dedicated to building a long-term relationship that isn't only transactional.

Onboarding Email Template

Every business' template is going to look a little different with unique elements and wording, but they should all contain a few basic elements.

- A welcome note
- How their purchase will meet their needs
- What to expect during the onboarding process

You should make your initial onboarding email relevant to your business and product but here's a great template to get you started:

Welcome, [customer name]

Hello [customer name],

Thanks for your recent purchase of [insert product or service name]! We're so happy you're here!

We created [insert product or service name] to help people like you [purpose of product or service], and we're so glad you chose us to meet your needs.

Over the next [insert onboarding timeline], we'll be sending you a variety of emails to help you get started with [insert product or service name]. We want to be sure you get the most benefit possible so be sure to add us to your contacts to ensure we get into your inbox.

We'll also be checking in with you to see how you're progressing. Please feel free to reach out with any questions or concerns.

We're so glad to have you in our community! Be sure to follow us on [insert social media channel] for the latest information and be a part of the fun!

Thanks,

[insert your name, company name, etc]

Creating an Onboarding Sequence

If you're creating an onboarding email sequence for the first time and aren't sure how to proceed, there are some basic steps you can take to ensure success. **Starting off, you'll want to deliver a warm welcome to your new clients and personalize your message to them as much as possible.**

You're also going to want to set up some way of monitoring inactive users so you can re-engage them if they stop reading or responding to your emails. This is all part of the plan to reduce churn and get them using your product regularly during the first 90 days.

You'll also want to be sure to optimize your emails for mobile users, as almost 50% of people read emails on their mobile device.

If you find your new clients not engaging with your emails as much as you wanted, consider doing some A/B testing. New designs, different copy, and timing can all be tested to get better results.

8 Tips for an Awesome Email Onboarding Sequence

1. Send a confirmation email first.

A successful onboarding sequence starts with confirming that your new subscriber or client is a real person with a legitimate address. The best way to accomplish this is by sending a short confirmation message to validate their email address.

A majority of your subscribers will complete this step pretty quickly but there will always be a few who will miss the email or forget to confirm. Set up a reminder email to be sure that they complete the confirmation.

The confirmation email doesn't have to be long or in depth, but it does need to have a clear call-to-action so the recipient knows exactly what to do to validate their email address.

2. Send an inviting welcome email.

Once your new subscriber or client has confirmed their email, you can get the onboarding process started. The welcome email is probably the most important part of your sequence, as it sets the tone for your entire onboarding process. Use your welcome email to make subscribers and clients eager to receive your next email.

Failure to create a good first impression is going to affect your open rates and click-through rates. A high-value welcome letter will turn people who are new subscribers into people who are loyal customers.

When your customers open your welcome email and believe that you can help them to reach their goals, it's much more likely that they will open additional emails from you.

3. Different sequences for engaged users and disengaged users.

One of the challenges of online marketing is dealing with subscribers who have different levels of engagement. Some will eagerly await the arrival of your next email while others may sign up or make a purchase but rarely open your emails.

Creating different sequences for active and inactive users is one way to account for this.

Active customers who regularly read your emails could receive a sequence that looks something like this:

- Encourage regular use
- Highlight key features or benefits
- Prompt a purchase
- Upsell or cross sell
- Share or refer

Inactive customers might receive emails that help to:

- Reaffirm your value proposition and encourage action
- Incentivize logging in or making a purchase
- Offer support
- Re-engage them with valuable content
- Win them back to the active side

Try segmenting your audience based on their actions (or inaction) so you can target them with appropriate emails. Inactive subscribers might respond if you highlight your value proposition.

4. Personalize for better engagement.

Personalizing your emails can increase engagement, drive higher open and click-through rates, as well as create an enhanced customer experience.

In order to personalize content, you'll need to know some data about your subscribers, and the more data you have the more personalized content you can create.

You can utilize both simple and more advanced personalization in your email sequences. Addressing your new client with their first and last name is one way to make the email more friendly. You can also consider sending emails from an employee or company address rather than a generic one.

5. Optimize emails for mobile users.

Almost half of all emails are opened on some sort of mobile device. Neglecting to optimize your email sequences for mobile devices will hurt your engagement. If users have to go home to their computer to open your email, they aren't going to do it.

Make sure your emails look good regardless of how they are opened. Pay attention to your visuals and copy. Simple images will load faster and your copy should be broken up with bolded text, bullet points, etc. Also, keep in mind that only a limited amount of characters are going to show up in your subject line.

6. Make sure your content highlights your CTA.

Without the right call-to-action, your new subscribers and clients are not going to know what they need to do next. They will read the email but fail to take advantage of your offer.

CTAs grab their attention and incentivize your reader to take action. In order to create a top-notch CTA, you'll need a combination of powerful copy and visuals.

Be sure to highlight the benefits of your product or service rather than the features to really drive home your CTA. Use images to make your information more understandable.

7. Always test your emails.

Everyone is going to be impacted differently by your emails. Testing your message will let you deliver content that engages them more effectively. The way to do this is by A/B testing. By A/B testing your emails, you can determine what is resonating more with your audience, which in turn will result in better open rates and click-throughs.

In order to test effectively, you want to create multiple variations of your email and send them to different segments of your audience. From there, you should be able to determine which one is getting the best engagement.

8. Be sure and provide tutorials and instructions.

New clients aren't going to be familiar with your products or services and may need a little help getting started. Providing them with instructions and tutorials will boost their confidence and help them to keep engaging.

FINAL THOUGHTS ON ONBOARDING CLIENTS

Client onboarding is an important part of your customer's journey with your brand. This guide is not the end-all of onboarding instructions. It's meant to give you ideas and help you to figure out what you want to communicate to your new clients as they are getting started.

Onboarding doesn't necessarily start when a purchase is made, it can start when a lead comes into contact with your brand. Every encounter is an opportunity for you to gather information so you can create an effective onboarding experience. Good onboarding leads to conversions, loyalty, and great customer relationships.